Tucked In HIM:

9 Days of Prayer for Headship and Covering

by

Keyon Blakes Bernal

Presented To:

Michele

From:

Date:

Expressions from the Heart:

Holy Holy Holy is the Lord God Almighty! The whole earth is full of His glory... This is what you release in the atmosphere! You are full of Holy Fire!

Tucked In HIM:

9 Days of Prayer for Headship and Covering

by

Keyon Blakes Bernal

Tucked in HIM: 9 Days of Prayer for Headship and Covering

by Keyon Blakes Bernal
© 2019

Published and Distributed by: Kingdom Business Kb

Print ISBN: 978-1-7330690-9-0

Project Editor: Pamela S Thibodeaux

First Printing: United States of America

Table of Contents

Dedication

I dedicate this prayer book first, to My Heavenly Father, PAPA, from whom ALL is made possible! You are my ultimate Headship and Covering. No words can express the depth of gratefulness I have for Your redemptive power in my life...You have made all the difference!

My grandmother, Gloria Sorina, who was a mighty prayer warrior and modeled endurance in prayer. From her, the mantle has been passed to me.

My husband, Dean Bernal Sr. My high priest, my one flesh covenant partner, my best friend, who, like my Heavenly Father, loves me, takes care of me and supports me beyond measure. You are AMAZING!

My Pastor, Ronald L. Mayo, who God used to develop and grow me in many areas, especially living in holiness, righteousness and prayer.

And to all who have led me and covered me, even when I didn't know it. THANK YOU! You are a part of this collaborative work!

In memory of Pastor Charles Robertson, a mighty man of Valor, who covered many, including me, and taught me to do everything from a position of strength! I honor you!

How to Use this Prayer Book

Congratulations and welcome! I'm so excited you decided to embark on this 9-day journey. I call it a journey because over the next 9 days or so, hopefully, you will experience a new place with God, as you set aside a little time to honor Him by praying for others in your life—especially those charged with leading.

Know this, as you set aside time to pray for others, their lives will be impacted and so will yours.

This journey may be filled with unexpected twists and curves, causing you to experience the full spectrum of human emotion. If so, hopefully, you will let it do, in you, whatever God has designed it to do. At the same time, your genuine prayers will pierce the heavens and prick the hearts and spirits of those you are praying for.

May any tears shed be cleansing and purifying, bringing you to repentance, forgiveness and deliverance where needed and forge a new freshness you've been longing for.

I pray you experience the joy of laughter as well, even if it is laughing at my personality as it comes through the pages. Speaking of which, you'll see an occasional ☺ or LOL! (which stands for laugh out loud) that you may not have ever seen in a professionally presented book.

I leave these in hopes of sharing my joy in the Lord with you. After all, Jesus said He came that our joy may be full. (*John 17:13 NASB*) I am authentically me and I pray for you to be free and authentically you. However it flows, just let it.

I'm all about flowing in the Spirit of God, so feel free to move through this as you feel led. If you want to skip around, go for it. Otherwise, for those who like structure, the introduction pages give some background information on how this prayer book was developed and insight into why 9 days and a few other interesting discoveries from my journey. Feel free to just follow the order of how things are laid out.

Note: There are some days with specific insights that will help with the prayer that follows. Also, as I was writing these prayers, every day was different. Sometimes God would drop a song in my spirit before praying, sometimes after. You'll see this reflected in the pages, as some days include a song before the prayer, and some include a song afterwards.

Tucked in HIM

I wrote it in the same order and pattern I experienced it. I just flowed as I was led, in my experience and journey, in writing the prayers from day to day.

Take notice that the prayers begin with praise and worship and some days there are specific prayers for you first, by design.

In Matthew 7:5, Jesus says we should remove the beam from our own eyes, then we can clearly see the sawdust in our brother's eye. This order is necessary because our prayers are more effective once we have put ourselves in a proper heart position, removing our beams and any hinderances first, through repentance and praise. This also sets our spirits in the right direction and invites God in.

Included are pages to journal or make notes if you so desire.

This is now your journey. I invite you in, connect your hand to Jesus' hand, and step back to allow you and Your Savior to walk, dance, prance, or maybe even stumble through the next 9 days. I am praying for you.

Yours in Christ,
Keyon

Introduction

I just *love* telling stories! Once I realized that, I affectionately began calling myself a storyteller. The good kind. Not one of those who make up fictional tales, but one of Truth–the truth of my life's experiences with God through Christ. These are the stories I just *love* to tell with *all* of the details, so the listener can picture the scenes in their mind. Like a movie! Yes, I *love* movies too. ☺

I preface with this statement because I'm going to tell you a short story of how these prayers were birthed, and to give a little context of what is contained in the pages to come.

Earlier this year (2018) I noticed a pattern of fasting God had begun to establish in me. I'd wake before dawn, at my set time to meet God in my prayer closet, which I now call my "Tent of Meeting." The place–the dark, quiet, intimate, undistracted place where I long to go every morning and meet with God and encounter His presence. Then the day would progress from there...morning chats with my hubby, workouts, errands, cooking and whatever lay ahead that God wanted me to do. This is my pattern.

Throughout the day, I remained in a spirit of

prayer–my heart lifted to God, looking for Him in every moment, around every corner, at every turn. God would stop me in my driveway or shift me to sit near the lake. He'd show up and tell me to stop wherever I was, and pray and intercede on behalf of others.

Going through the day in this state, I'd look up and it would be after 2:00 pm and I would just have a "knowing" to keep praying and fasting until 3:00 pm. I'd just "walk" into fasting.

I believe that's the way life happens when we truly walk with Jesus. We have daily plans, but we remain open, and leave space for Him to enter into those plans, disrupting them if necessary, and walk us to the place and state in which He wants us to be.

Initially, at the onset of the day, fasting wasn't a plan, intent, nor a direction-it just happened. I'd like to note that I wasn't going about the day doing my normal daily routine and *forgot* to eat, then made the choice to call it a fast.

I was literally and consciously in a spirit of prayer and worship, which is what caused me to not even think of food. So, if you happen to skip breakfast and lunch because you got busy at work or engulfed in the day's demands, don't go labeling that a spiritual fast, *LOL!*

As my pastor says, "fasting without prayer is just fasting, but fasting coupled with prayer will cause you to hear the voice of God!"

To add an interesting dynamic, this pattern typically happened on Fridays and started happening so often, I had to stop and ask God what was up with *this?!*

All of these little nuances struck me, and got my attention enough to seek the Lord for insight into the purpose of this particular pattern. Clearly, none of this was happenstance or coincidence.

I don't believe in coincidences.

So, I searched high and low for significance of prayer at the 3:00 pm hour. I found a lot on 3:00 am, but nothing on 3:00 pm, which in this moment is making me giggle because of what God had planned and how He unveiled what I was seeking.

Let's be honest here, in actuality, God set me up to seek this information in the first place...He's my Dad, He knows me. So, He left *just* enough breadcrumbs, in *just* the right places, knowing I would recognize the pattern and follow the trail, going on a God ordained search to discover the hidden treasure He planted for me to find.

He knows you too. God is so AMAZINGLY COOL!

Exasperated with coming up short on my search, I said, "Ok Lord, You know what I'm looking for, so when You're ready for me to discover it, show me." I left it with Him and moved on.

A few days later, while reading my devotional, a phenomenal book called *The Book of Mysteries*, by Jonathan Cahn, my mouth fell open, I hung my head and then looked up and said, "Lord, You are something else! I'm undone by YOU!!!"

I just "happened" to read about the significance of Fridays and 3:00 pm in that book, **after** this fasting pattern clearly emerged!

Did I say I don't believe in coincidences?

Let's start with unveiling the Friday mystery:

"'As the Sabbath approaches," said the teacher, "the observant among the children of Israel must finish up all their work..."

The Sabbath is called the Sabbath not because of a day, but because of an event, an act of God. As it is written, 'God ended His work, which He had done, and He rested on the seventh day from all His work which He had done.' Behind the word rested is the Hebrew word shevat. Shevat means to cease. On the seventh day God ceased...

*And the timing of that ceasing would have to be linked to the timing of the Sabbath. It was **Friday afternoon**, the end of the sixth day...and as in the beginning, the sixth day was the day of the completion of God's labors. So the labors of God were completed on the cross...and then on the cross...He ceased.'" (**emphasis mine**)*

Let's make it plain and practical, connecting some pieces together. Friday is the sixth day of the week. So, on Friday afternoon, the people of God and all who observed the Sabbath ceased from their labors until Saturday evening at sundown. That was their rest.

Genesis 2:2-3 is where we find God doing the same thing in the Creation story. He worked, labored for six days creating the earth, then rested on the seventh day. On Friday afternoon, the work was done, it was "finished."

In view of this, I could clearly see the

significance of why I felt led into fasting on Fridays.

Now let's unveil the 3:00 pm mystery:

"So the morning lamb was offered up at the third hour... which is what time?"
"Nine in the morning. And when was Messiah crucified?... Nine in the morning, the same hour. So as the morning lamb was slain on the altar..."
"The lamb of God was lifted up on the altar of the cross..."

*"And the evening lamb," I said, "at the **ninth hour**, what time was that?"*
*"**Three in the afternoon**," he said, "the same hour Messiah died on the cross..."* (**emphasis mine**)

Did you catch that?!

The 9th hour, which is 3:00 pm, is the hour when Jesus said, "It is finished," and gave up His spirit and died for the sins of the world!

If there was an emoji I could use right here to express how I feel when writing this, I'd fill the page up!!!

Let's put it all together:

Jesus did the work He came to do and fulfilled His earthly ministry. When it was done, like God in the Creation story, He brought His work to completion on Friday, the sixth day.

On that day, at the 9th hour (3:00 pm), He said, "It is finished" and gave up His spirit. He *ceased* from His labors on earth for the salvation of mankind, so the Holy Spirit would be released! HALLELUJAH! THANK YOU, JESUS!!!

I was praying and fasting, that was and is my work—"laboring" through fasting. When it was done as I was led, like God in the Creation story, I brought my work to completion on Friday, the sixth day. On that day, at the 9th hour, 3:00 pm, it was finished, and I released it to God.

I laid my petitions down before the Lord and labored during the time of labor, I planted seeds in the season of planting. For when the work, the labor I was called to do at that time, was complete, I ceased.

On the same day of the week and the same time my Savior said, "It is finished!" At His leading and in His shadow and image, so did I!

I venture to say, **this is significant!**

This was unbeknownst to me when I went on the search for a 3:00 pm connection. I clearly had no idea of the depth of this until the moment of unveiling. Just writing and reliving the gravity of this revelation...**Wow!**

I need a moment to Selah (stop, pause and think about it).

My heartbeat has increased and I am literally shaking my head while typing! I'll say this now and maybe many more times: I AM UNDONE AND RUINED BY GOD AND I LOVE IT!!!

This is what I call "the beyond." It blows my mind every time I read this or think about it. Yes, He has ruined me. Status Quo and the ordinary won't cut it for me anymore. The more He gives me and shows me, keeps me thirsting for more—more of HIM, more of His heart, more of the BEYOND! The place that's deep and far out in Him, beyond this world, beyond our comprehension—and God, being the God He is, never disappoints.

Friends, these moments and times, when I just

"happened" to fall into such experiences...is the place these prayers and this book was birthed out of.

I love stating that I just "happened" to "fall" or "walk" into moments because it makes it clear that this was obviously not my doing, but *all* God's. It's humbling and reminds me of the Apostle Paul's words in *Ephesians 2.* Paul was speaking of salvation, but the words ring true and apply here for me as well...

*"and that not of yourselves, it is a gift of God, not as a result of works, so that **no one may boast**." (v.8b-9 NABS) (**emphasis mine**)*

I have no reason to boast, but ***every*** reason to give all of the glory where it belongs—to God!

One day in particular, July 16, 2018, this same pattern began to emerge as I exited the Tent of Meeting. I could sense where this day was going, so I flowed with God and remained in a spirit of fasting and praying as I went about my daily business at home.

I was praying in the spirit (Romans 8:26-27) and putting the sheets on our massage table. As I lifted each sheet up and watched it flow down and cover the next, it was like I could see and hear the word "covering" in my spirit. I continued to pray and as always, anointed each sheet with Frankincense and Myrrh.

I paused and pondered for a second as words in English began to flow out of my mouth. I put the face cover over the head piece and heard "headship." I paused again and said, "Ok God," and then put the final piece, a healing blanket, on the table. At this point Headship and Covering was sealed in my spirit and I felt I had to stop immediately and write down the prayer I was hearing.

When I finished writing the prayer down, I felt led to share with a few intercessors and ask if they would pray it with me over Headship and Covering that day, and they did.

I didn't think anything more about it, had no idea or expectation of anything else. As far as I was concerned, that was it. This is an over used phrase, albeit true...BUT GOD!

The next day, I woke up and went about my daily prayer, devotional and meditation time with God and out of nowhere, came another prompting for Headship & Covering, so I wrote down what was coming to me. I said, "Ok God, is this a pattern? If so, do whatever You want. I'll obey; just let me hear you *clearly*."

For the next seven consecutive days, the same type of thing happened. My devotional scripture, or a scripture from another source I read that day, had something about leadership that would trigger a prayer for Headship and Covering and I wrote down what I heard. On day 9 as you'll see, the closing to the prayer was Jesus' declaration on the cross at the 9th hour, "***It is finished***."

In that moment, I paused, looked up and said, "Lord, are You saying this is the end of this journey? Is this the end of these prayers? Let me hear You clearly!" *Or not,* I thought with a laugh. Even now I chuckle, knowing I sometimes feel I'm done with a matter or subject and God, with His infinite sense of humor, is just beginning or has more in store for me. And sometimes, like in this case, His lack of an answer *was* His answer.

The next day, I moved on in my normal fashion, open to whatever and however God wanted to move and/or speak, with no expectation other than Him showing up. I mean, this is His party and I'm just open to His flow and excited to be invited into His company.

God never answered my question with an emphatic yes or no. However, the absence of receiving a prayer or any inclination of Headship, Covering or anything relating to leadership at all was emphatically clear enough. Since nothing so specific or similar came to me, I got it. He said it and meant what He said – *"It is finished!"*

Why 9 Days?

"Because God said so" is my ultimate answer ☺.

If you read the last paragraph, my saying this makes perfect sense! Typically, this is my stand and that's good enough for me. However, since He created us, God knows all of His children so well and He knew that answer wouldn't suffice for everyone. Therefore, He decided to humor us with a little more information on *the why*.

God is a very strategic God, who wastes *nothing*. Nothing He does is arbitrary or by happenstance. Therefore, I'm a big believer in God speaking to His people through *anything* and *everything* He chooses, for He made **all** things. (*John 1:3* NASB) And I would reckon to say since the Lord opened a donkey's mouth and caused it to speak; He can speak through anything else! *Numbers 22:28 (*NASB)

Numbers are very significant to God and He uses them in many ways to speak to us. For our intended purpose in this prayer book, numbers speak–the number 9 in particular.

Biblically, 9 represents several things. There are:

* 9 fruits of the Spirit *(Galatians 5:22)*
* 9 gifts of the Spirit *(1 Corinthians 12:4)*
* 9 is synonymous with birth, as the 9th month is when a woman gives birth and is the end of pregnancy, while at the same time the beginning of new life

As it pertains to us and this 9-day journey, the book of Acts gives us some insight into the number 9 as representing prayer and intercession.

*Acts 3:1 NASB says, "Now Peter and John were going up to the temple at the **9th hour**, the hour of prayer." (**emphasis mine**)*

And Cornelius said, *"Four days ago to this hour, I was praying in my house during the **9th hour**; and behold, a man stood before me in shining garments." (Acts 10:30 NASB **emphasis mine**)*

Peter says the 9th hour is the hour of prayer, while at the 9th hour while praying, Cornelius saw a heavenly being. That's pretty cool and pretty obvious in pointing to the significance of the number 9.

By the way, remember, not too long ago we

unveiled that I was led into fasting and praying until 3:00 pm or the 9th hour, the hour of prayer. Selah.

This also reveals hints into some of God's character and how He operates using time and numbers.

God even reveals the significance of the number 9 and its connection to prayer, in its very shape. Take another look at the illustration on the cover of this book, a man tucked within HIM in the humble position of prayer.

I'll share this just for kicks. Some friends that looked at the illustration also said it looks like a man, yet a baby in a womb. How befitting. When we are tucked in God, through Christ, in the humble position of prayer, aren't we going before Him like little children? (*Matthew 18:2-3 NASB*)

After all, He is our Heavenly Father. And from this position of humility and power, our prayers birth much fruit!

By the way, I'm sure you guessed it; I am a numbers girl/geek. ☺

Why Headship and Covering?

Sharing my understanding of Headship and Covering before ensuing to the actual prayers, is the final piece of the puzzle

I don't believe God wants us blindly praying and following along in a prayer book with no understanding, ergo no heart involvement. He created every facet of our bodies wonderfully and that includes our minds.

When we have understanding and insight into things, they can then flow through the mind and go straight to our hearts. God's not interested in our many empty words. He's interested in the words that are birthed in, and come from, our hearts, and that, many times, start with understanding. *(Proverbs 4:7 NET Bible)*

Now if you happen to be like me, following the sequential order of things, you started at the beginning and have read everything in order up to this point. That means you have a good foundational background, insight, and understanding for moving forward. Good job! Otherwise, if you happen to be like my husband, you will probably never see this part because you totally skipped over the intro, the background and already prayed all of the prayers. It's all good, bless your heart. God knows. ☺

Who knows, maybe a few months later, you're just seeing the intro or your spouse or a friend finds it interesting, and since they know you, they decided to read it to you, so you won't miss out. This is all good too, that's how the "body" works...together, embracing our differences. LOL!

Back to the serious stuff. Or as our tour guide on our pilgrimage in Israel would say "off the silly note."

Of all the things and people we can pray for, why pray specifically for Headship and Covering? What is the significance? Why does it matter?

We remember that God is a God of order and hierarchy. He designed and established every family with an order. Whether it is individual families or the unified family of the Body of Christ, His order and establishment provide covering, as in protection and leadership for us, His children.

In the creation of humankind, God first created Adam, second Eve, third, from them came their children. Adam was headship. *(Genesis 2:7, 18, 21-22; 1 Corinthians 11:3)*

When I say Headship, I'm referring to leadership, which looks very different in different situations and environments. We don't serve a cookie cutter type God. In a church, it's the Pastor, in a marriage, it's the husband, (married ladies, don't flinch, just pray). You are not the head...Sorry, not sorry. I'm laughing here and I pray you're laughing with me. See *Ephesians 5:22-33* for further insight on this.

In a single parent home, where mom is the leader, Headship is mom. In a classroom, Headship belongs to the teacher, and so on. Ultimately above pastor, husband, mom, teachers, etc., JESUS is the head. Therefore, every leader has to answer to the Lord Jesus Christ who is head and leader over the Body of Christ. They have to give an account of how they lead those God entrusted to them to steward.

Everyone can have opinions and a voice, but everyone can't be in charge. That would lend to chaos, division and a house in shambles. A house divided against itself cannot stand; it falls. *(Mark 3:25, Luke 11:17)* There has to be a delegated authority, that when all is said and done, that position or office is respected to make the final decision. Good reason for us to pray for our leaders!

In scripture, from the beginning, whether it was with Adam and Eve or in the era of the Judges or the Kings, there has always been Headship. The judges and the kings, these brave leaders had advisors to help guide them. They listened and considered the opinions and/or advice of their support system, but when it came down to it, with all things considered, the chosen leader had to make the final call. Think about it, that's a lot of responsibility!

In the days when there were no judges nor kings, no leadership, the bible says every man did what he thought was right in his own sight and it was a colossal mess! *(Judges 21:25, Judges 21-22* tells the story*)*

A friend of ours has a funny, but true saying that applies here: *"Anything with no head is dead and anything with two heads is a mess."* When there are two chiefs, we have confusion and those who follow don't know which leader to listen to. So, when the head listens, considers, seeks the Lord and makes one final decision for the team, no one is confused, and everyone can flow in the same direction, no division.

This is another great reason to pray for our leaders *and* those following. We need to pray for them to seek the Lord and have the ability to hear

Him and walk in obedience. We also need to make sure as followers, our hearts are right and trusting God ourselves.

Otherwise, when decisions are made that we don't agree with, we can very easily harbor resentment, bitterness and anger. On the surface it may look like we're going along with the leader's decision, but our hearts are secretly divided. This is very, very dangerous. It's a breeding ground for the enemy to come in, kill, steal and destroy. *(John 10:10 NASB)*

This is yet another critical reason to pray for Headship and Covering. When we sincerely pray for our leaders and trust and believe that God hears our prayers, we can align ourselves with leadership, even when we don't agree or see the vision they see, because we know through prayer, God is ultimately in control. This keeps us united with pure hearts. This pleases God.

We weren't designed to do life alone, yet many times, it's a lonely and heavy road being the head. But we can help! How? I'm so glad you asked.

Let's consider Moses' plight. He was charged with the great responsibility of leading the entire nation of Israel out of Egypt into freedom from slavery. We're talking about millions of people in the wilderness, the desert. Hot, tired, hungry and free, but confused and still mentally bound.

God sent the miraculous Manna from heaven for them to eat daily and that wasn't good enough. They wanted the food they had in Egypt when they were slaves. *(Numbers 11)* If you haven't read it, check out the book of Exodus for the full riveting story.

What does this kind of combination lead to? Millions of people ungratefully complaining to the leader. My my my...who does that sound like at one time or another? Yep...us!

Moses got so frustrated and cried out to God, asking why God handed him these people *(Numbers 11:11)*. The people were burdensome to him! Wow, when we are ungrateful and whine and cry about childish, foolish things we can be a burden to our leaders–the very ones we depend on to guide us.

Imagine how challenging it must be to lead people like this. If you have children or family members you've helped, how does it feel when they behave this way?!?

I don't know about you, but I don't want to be that person. Lord, forgive me in this moment for any and every time this was me! As much as is possible, I want to be helpful to all of the leaders in my life. Like Joel Osteen says, "I want to be powerful, not pitiful." We don't have to be leaders to embody this statement. We can be powerful followers and help make the load a little lighter on all of our leaders in many ways, especially through the support of prayer.

You might be a leader in your own right, but you're a leader under a leader, just like the sheets on my massage table or the sheets on your bed. We don't typically use one sheet, there are layers.

First the foundation is the mattress which is *covered* by a fitted sheet; the fitted sheet is *covered* by a flat sheet. In some cases, the flat sheet is *covered* by a coverlet and the coverlet is *covered* by a blanket. Each layer, each leader, needs support and covering.

As a leader, when Moses got tired, he needed Aaron and Hur to hold up his hands in battle for support *(Exodus 17:12)*. Today is no different. You as a leader *and* your leader all need support. When you're in the position of the follower, treat your leaders how you want to be treated.

Remember the saying, anything with no head is dead, anything with two heads is a mess? If we don't have proper leadership, everything under that leader's authority is affected. If leadership is confused, everyone following that leader will, in some way, walk unsure. Yes, exactly...a mess!

This affects generations!

We need our Headship strong, vibrant, refreshed and revived so they can clearly hear from the Lord and lead us in His ways. We don't want them tired, frustrated and burdened down. There's no joy in that for them or for us. This leaves everyone miserable. We must do our part and support them every time the Lord leads us to and this prayer book is one easy way to do so.

A Little note on Covering

Some of you surely understand Headship, but maybe have a little question mark where Covering is concerned. For insight and clarity, I'd like us to look at Psalm 91:1-4.

In the version of the bible I use a lot, NASB, this psalm is titled "Security of the One Who Trusts in the LORD":

"He who dwells in the shelter of the Most High will abide in the shadow of the Almighty.

I will say to the Lord, "My refuge and my fortress, My God, in whom I trust!"

For it is He who delivers you from the snare of the trapper and from the deadly pestilence.

*He will **cover** you with His pinions (feathers, wings), and under His wings you may seek refuge;*

His faithfulness is a shield and bulwark (something surrounding a person, shield)."
(emphasis mine)

As you can see these verses are about

protection. More specifically when we look at the word covering in its Hebraic origin, (covering sometimes can be referred to as canopy) the Hebrew word is yasek, which literally means fence in, cover over, protect, defense, hedge in, to block, overshadow, stop the approach. Hallelujah!!!

This is what covering in prayer produces! So those who are leaders and cover you in prayer are providing protection, a form of defense, hedging you in safety, blocking and even stopping the approach of the enemy coming toward your life.

The people who are considered Covering, are those on the spiritual battlefield, warring for you and me. In light of this, from a spiritual perspective, they are just like our military troops who fight for our physical protection everyday. Our Covering fights for our spiritual, physical, emotional and mental protection. Therefore, they need someone covering and supporting them as well.

When we are uncovered, it's like Eve coming in contact with the serpent. She was unprotected, no shield around her, nothing to block or stop the serpent's approach. If her covering, Adam, was on point and actually covering her, looking out for her best interest, protecting her, surely, he would've shut the enemy down when she missed it.

Yes, God is ultimately the covering for everyone, but there is a hierarchy and God gave that job to Adam. And like a great Father, He allowed this to happen as a lesson to humankind. If we look at the heart of the matter, this can teach us, in a very real sense, what the ramifications are when there is lack of clarity, disobedience and when we get out of order and out of position. This is applied to both Adam and Eve and it applies to all of us as well.

Ladies, I know, when our husbands step in, sometimes we feel like we don't need or want them to. I'm sure if we're honest, in hindsight, many times we come to the realization that what we perceived as harm or a violation on their part was actually them protecting us. I can personally testify to this!

And men, although you are the head, God uses wives as your backup, your support. He gives insight where you might miss it, because you are human. It's OK; just learn to use the secret weapon in your arsenal.

One time my husband and I went to the altar for prayer concerning a business venture and our Pastor spoke a Word to us from the Lord. I'll never forget this. He told my husband, "When you miss it, she's going to catch it." What a simple, yet profound statement for teamwork in a marriage. He didn't usurp the authority my husband had; neither did he make me feel like I was second fiddle.

He gave both of us validity and support in our individual positions, yet as a team. Married couples, employees, and in relationships as a whole, we've got to get this understanding within our spirits. We need each other more than we realize. It's how God ordained us to live–in community together.

Nevertheless, *Covering* is referring to leadership, but not limited to leadership. Anyone who is a covering for someone else, in any sense, is considered here. If you're a brother or sister and you *cover* your siblings in prayer, in these pages, you are considered *Covering*.

If you consider yourself the lowest of the low in your workplace and don't think you have much value, (it's a lie), yet in your heart and your private time, you lift someone else up in prayer–maybe your supervisor. You are covering them. God sees and you have much value. This is also intended to *cover* you. These prayers are to *cover* the covers and the blanket on top of all the covers!

A few notes before we embark on this 9-day journey:

Just a reminder: Each day we will enter in prayer and into God's presence properly with praise and worship. There is power in our words, so we will speak aloud in the atmosphere who God is, to ourselves, the spirit realm, the enemy, the world and anyone or anything that would try to come against us with doubt.

When we begin to declare with our voices the attributes and character of God, not only do our spirits line up and get set on fire, but our faith builds up. God is moved and shows up, for He is enthroned, He sits on and is in the midst of, the praises of His people. *(Psalm 22:3 NLT)*

As previously stated, some days you will see sections that include insight into the area we will target in prayer. This is to help with deeper understanding in these areas.

There are also some days where you will see a song suggested. These are days when the Lord dropped these songs in my spirit that connect with the prayer for that day. Sometimes the song will be at the beginning and sometimes it will be at the end. It is positioned in the place God gave it to me and so, in like manner, I pass it on to you.

Finally, these prayers are meant to be prayed aloud, not just read. Make them personal. If you are praying these prayers with someone, feel free to say "we" in the places where it says "I" and say the names of those you are praying for wherever you feel led.

Give voice and power to your prayers with a spirit of declaration. Here we imitate our Heavenly Father. In His image, as in the creation story, call into being that which does not exist. *(Romans 4:17 NASB)*

"In the beginning God created the heavens and the earth. The earth was *formless and void*, and *darkness* was over the surface of the deep, and the Spirit of God was moving over the surface of the waters. Then God **said**, "Let there be light"; and there was light." Gen 1:1-3 NASB (**emphasis mine)**

So, pray them aloud with fervency and boldness, then take notice, because God will show up and He will answer.

Let's pray...

Father, thank You for who You are in my life

and thank You for walking with me and bringing me to this point and place at this moment. I desire to bless You, be pleasing to You and walk in Your will and Your ways. I surrender my will, my rights and all control to You. I am open, teach me.

I don't want to be burdensome to my Headship, I want to be like Aaron and Hur, the support system that holds up their arms in tough times and share in the joys and victories of high times.

I welcome You into this journey. Have Your way completely. I desire to be used by You; to be a fresh wind of encouragement, the wind beneath the wings of my leaders as they lead families in the body of Christ—at home, work and in every entity of life! Come Holy Spirit. In Jesus' Name I pray. AMEN!

DAY 1: *The Foundation*

Praise and Worship:

ABBA FATHER, I declare at the onset of these prayers, as the foundation, that You are *the* Good Good Father and You've been better than good to me and I say THANK YOU! I worship You in this moment, honoring You and lifting Your name and Your name alone, on high! You, Lord, are the Ultimate, Supreme, the first and the last, the beginning and the end of everything.

Prayer:

Lord, with a humble and repentant heart, I come. I repent for everything I've done that hasn't been pleasing in Your sight. Sins I've been aware of and those I'm not aware of, I humbly ask for Your forgiveness and revelation into where I need to change.

Father, I don't want anything to hinder my prayers, so create in me a clean heart and renew within me a right spirit. Purge me from my wrong ways of thinking, acting and being, and teach me to walk, to live uprightly before You, that I may be found pleasing in Your sight. May my prayers be effective in the heavens and the earth.

I bring my Headship, and anyone who has been Covering me in the spirit, unto You through Jesus Christ, the Ultimate Covering!

Hide them in the cleft of the Rock, for Under the shadow of Your wings they find comfort, like a soft, warm blanket of security and assuredness. I cover and pray healing for wounds of the soul and heart—all the way from the womb. I declare these things are dead! I pray for rest for their minds, peace in their hearts and restoration of their souls—TOTAL HEALING—in mind, body and spirit.

I decree divine alignment for their lives and Kingdom assignments. As this divine, strategic, alignment takes place, and the *total* healing that emanates from Christ's covering heals and delivers them deep within, the healing then further emanates from *Headship* and *Covering* to those they are covering in Jesus' Name!

Then the revolution and flow of Restoration and *total healing* will take place in the BODY of Christ! I decree it by faith, by the Blood and in the Name of Jesus, the Christ! AMEN, SO BE IT!

Psalm 51, Psalm 57:5, Revelation 21:6, 1 Corinthians 11:3, Exodus 33:22, Psalm 36:7, Malachi 4:2, Acts 10:38

Tucked in HIM

Heart Notes, Insights, Revelations

_____

_____

_____

_____

_____

_____

_____

_____

_____

_____

_____

_____

Heart Notes, Insights, Revelations

_____

_____

_____

_____

_____

_____

_____

_____

_____

_____

_____

_____

DAY 2: *Hitting the Bullseye*

Praise and Worship:

Father, I never skip an opportunity to give Your name praise! I shout Hallelujah to the King of Kings and the Lord of Lords! In this moment, it doesn't matter if I feel like it and it doesn't matter what things look like, because I look to You.

When I lift my eyes to the hills, I see You and I am ushered into the gravitational pull of heaven to worship! When my eyes and heart behold You, all I can say is Hallelujah! You are worthy to be praised!

Prayer:

From this place of praise, seated in heavenly places, I come with the fire of the Holy Spirit in my mouth, like a flaming sword. I come in the strength of the Lord my God, knowing by faith, when I decree a thing it shall be, it will be, it IS established because I am praying in agreement with Your Word, Your heart, Your Spirit!

I put my warfare clothes on, my full armor of God, so that I am able to stand firm against the schemes of the devil. For this battle, this struggle is not against human beings, but with the highest principalities and authorities operating in rebellion under the heavenly realms, against evil spirits that hold this world in bondage.

Therefore, I must wear all the armor that You provide so I am protected as I confront the slanderer, for I and my Headship and Covering are destined for all things, and we will rise victorious.

So then, I take my stand! Fastening the Truth of God's Word around my waist like a belt, I put on God's approval as my breastplate of righteousness and my shoes are on so that I am ready to spread the Good News that gives peace.

I take my Christian faith as a shield, for with it I can put out all the flaming arrows of the evil one. Also, I take salvation as my helmet and the Word of God as the sword that the Spirit supplies.

I come annihilating every enemy that would rear its head against my Headship and Covering. I bind powers and principalities, spiritual wickedness in high places, and render them null, void, inoperative, ineffective, of no avail, and stripped of power! I rise up, not by power, not by might, but by the Spirit of the Living God. As an end time warrior in this dispensation I fight, I wage war, and I am on the offense!

Lord, give my leaders new strategies, tactics and the ability to see the enemy like never before. Even as the enemy tries to move fast and elude their line of sight, give my Headship sights like a hunter with a scope on his rifle–lined up and locked in–leaving no way of escape for the enemy. No more wasting energy, swatting needlessly, constantly missing and getting frustrated...that time has come to an end!

As a sniper in the realm of the spirit, my Headship and Covering lies in wait for the enemy–patient, focused–and in the perfect moment, takes them out with one shot! The enemy is annihilated in every area of their lives, in Jesus' Name!

Psalm 7:17; Revelation 19:16; Psalm 121:1; Revelation 19:1; Psalm 96:4; Ephesians 2:6; Acts 2:3-4; Psalm 28:7; Ephesians 6:11-13 TPT; Ephesians 6:14-17 GW; Job 22:28; John 14:14; Deuteronomy 7:2; Matthew 18:18; Ephesians 6:12; Luke 10:19; Zechariah 4:6; Ephesians 6:10-18; Isaiah 43:19; Jeremiah 11:18; Jeremiah 48:8; 1 Corinthians 9:27

Heart Notes, Insights, Revelations

Heart Notes, Insights, Revelations

_____

_____

_____

_____

_____

_____

_____

_____

_____

_____

_____

_____

_____

_____

Day 3: *Today is ROOT OUT Day!*

Praise and Worship:

I lift up the name of Jesus and praise You, Lord, for You are good and Your mercy endures forever! All blessings flow from You and You alone. I set my heart on You and Your Kingdom.

Thank You for the blessing of You! Thank You for Jesus' life and sacrifice on my behalf. Thank You for revealing Yourself to me and desiring a relationship with me, and in turn, I desire a closer walk with You. I desire to sit with You. I just want YOU! Come and sup with me Lord. More than anything else, I long for Your presence.

Prayer:

Father, Your Word says that only he with clean hands and a pure heart can ascend to Your holy hill. I don't want anything standing in the way of my alignment with You or hindering my prayers. Therefore, I loose the Spirit of God to go deep within me, as well as Headship and Covering, and do a cleansing work—rooting out dead things that are hiding and taking up space reserved for the "new" in our lives. Build my leaders' strength by pruning and plucking those things and people from their lives that no longer serve Your purpose in their assignment.

Father, I ask You to deal not only with obvious things, but those things that are hard to perceive, because they hurt, not by causing more injury, but by hindering progress. Holy Spirit, move through their lives like a mighty, rushing wind, like the waves and roar of the ocean. You are unstoppable and no foe can stand against You!

Clean hands and pure hearts are what I'm crying out for. As You wash clean those things that have been killed, I pray for an outpouring and infilling of the Spirit to touch the dry ground where dead things once lay, and make the ground fertile, that my Headship and Covering may bear much fruit.

I pray for You, Lord, to lead them in preparation to receive the latter rain! I pray for the manifestation of Pentecost to take place in each soul and spirit. I am calling forth fruit! As this happens personally within Headship and Covering, it is going to flow and spread to the BODY of Christ like a wildfire—In Jesus' Name!

Psalm 136:1; James 1:17; John 3:16; Psalm 19:1-4; Romans 1:20; Zephaniah 3:17; Psalm 42:1; Psalm 24:3-4; 2 Corinthians 10:5; 1 Peter 3:7; Matthew 18:18; 1 John 1:9; Romans 8:6; Jeremiah 1:10; Daniel 2:22; Isaiah 40:29; John 15:2; Acts 2:2; Psalm 89:9; 2 Chronicles 20:6; 2 Timothy 1:7; Psalm 105:24; John 15:8; Joel 2:23; Acts 2:1-4; 37-47

Heart Notes, Insights, Revelations

_____

_____

_____

_____

_____

_____

_____

_____

_____

_____

_____

_____

Heart Notes, Insights, Revelations

_____

_____

_____

_____

_____

_____

_____

_____

_____

_____

_____

_____

_____

Day 4: *NO Neutrality*

Praise and Worship:

Father, You said, *"Let there be lights in the expanse of the heavens to separate the day from the night, and let them be for signs and for seasons and for days and years; and let them be for lights in the expanse of the heavens to give light on the earth"*; and so it was.

Lord, You made the two great lights, the greater light to govern the day, and the lesser light to govern the night; You made the stars also and You placed them in the expanse of the heavens to give light on the earth, and to govern the day and the night, and to separate the light from the darkness; and You saw that it was good and You completed the fourth day of creation.

Who wouldn't serve and praise a God like You? With all power in Your hands, You spoke it and it was so. Let people of this world magnify You, Lord, and let us all exalt Your name together! For there is none like You in all the earth. You are the One and True Living God! When all other gods required sacrifice, You, Yourself became my Sacrifice. Oh, what a LOVE!

Thank You Father, thank You for coming to rescue me. Thank You for becoming sin for me. You're the same God who set the stars in the sky and told them to shine, yet You humbled Yourself for me! You're a mind-blowing God, Hallelujah!

If I had 10,000 tongues, I still couldn't praise You enough. Father, I know before I even pray, You're moving right now, just because I'm coming before You with praise and worship unto Your Holy, Magnificent, Unparalleled Name! So, I thank You right now for what You're doing *while* I worship, *while* I worship, *while* I worship YOU!

Prayer:

With this kind of love shed abroad for us, Lord I come boldly declaring over Headship and Covering *no neutrality!* You don't deserve our love and commitment to be dissected and split. You don't deserve leftovers. You deserve the first fruits of all hearts, souls and minds, and the first fruits of all strength! You don't deserve divided alliances.

I decree the hearts and minds of my Headship and Covering are set like flint on You and You alone, on Your will and Your will only. They choose light and root out any darkness, compromise, or *any* ungodly thing that still exists, no matter how small—*no middle ground!*

As they continue to walk in the realm of *no neutrality,* give them the increased ability to discern times and seasons, like the tribe of Issachar, so they can move in sync and in sequence with You.

As You move in their lives and position them, recognizing this is a large task for them to lead Your people, and because You are a God of balance, I ask for rest and support for them as well. Lord, send the right people at the right time to be willing to step in, like Aaron and Hur did for Moses.

When you send them, help Headship to discern and be humble enough to know they can't do it on their own, receive the help, and take rest when You extend Your hand to offer it.

I bind up and root out fear and intimidation of someone taking their place, and loose security in their position in the Kingdom. I root up and cast out pride and disobedience, and loose humility and a spirit of obedience over them and in them. Like King David, they are Headship and Covering after Your Own Heart, Lord! In Jesus' Name!

Song: Blessing and Cursing

Spoken Word By John Paul Jackson

Genesis 1:14-19; Matthew 28:18; Psalm 34:3; Jeremiah 10:6; John 17:3; Jeremiah 10:10; 1 John 2:2; Philippians 2:8; Matthew 6:8; Exodus 23:25; Acts 16:25; Romans 5:5; Hebrews 4:16; Joshua 24:15; Revelation 3:15-16; Nehemiah 10:35-39; Deuteronomy 11:18; John 8:12; Romans 13:14; 2 Corinthians 6:14-15; 1 Chronicles 12:32; 1 Kings 19:4-8; Exodus 17:12; 2 Timothy 1:7; 1 John 4:18; James 4:6; 1 Peter 5:5; Deuteronomy 5:33; 1 Samuel 13:14

Heart Notes, Insights, Revelations

_____

_____

_____

_____

_____

_____

_____

_____

_____

_____

_____

_____

Heart Notes, Insights, Revelations

_____

_____

_____

_____

_____

_____

_____

_____

_____

_____

_____

_____

Day 5: *Wisdom and Discernment*

Insight:

There are times when we are tired and the Lord says rest, but we can't hear His voice for various reasons. We make up our minds that we must do a litany of things that God may not be telling us to do. Because we are running on empty and need recovery time with Him, we may be in the danger zone and God sends warning. We must heed the signs.

Yet there are times when we are tired and feel we are ready to rest and the Lord still requires more, as He did of the fishermen in Luke chapter 5.

They fished all night, caught nothing and were ready to be done for the day, yet Jesus said, *"Cast your nets into the deep."* They were sensitive to the Master's voice and moved in obedience then the overflow miracle manifested!

The Lord longs to manifest "overflow miracles" in and through Headship and Covering, as well as the Body of Christ, but we must be sensitive to the Father's voice to know when and how to flow and walk in obedience, which sometimes requires rest and other times, require pushing beyond ourselves. The only way to know is to get tucked in Him, ask and listen for His response.

Praise and Worship:

Song: Blessings and Honor (*Psalm 45:6*)
By: Fred Hammond and Radical for Christ

Blessings and honor Oh God! Glory and Power Oh God! Dominion Forever! Let my heart cry this today in worship as I bow my heart before the King of Kings and the Lord of Lords! Blessings and honor Oh God! Glory and Power Oh God! Dominion Forever!

I worship You. You are my Redeemer. You are my Forever. You are my Truth. You are my Wisdom. You are my Righteousness. You are my Everything! You are my Voice. You are my Peace. You are my Quiet. You are my EVERYTHING! I owe You praise and pure worship for Who You Are—the Great I AM!

I cry with the angels, Holy Holy Holy is the Lord God Almighty, who was, is and is to come!

Blessings and honor Oh God! Glory and Power Oh God! Dominion Forever!

Prayer:

Father, my prayer today is simply for wisdom and discernment, as well as sensitive ears for Headship and Covering. Lord help them to know very specifically when You are saying push–push past the tiredness and cast your nets into the "deep" and watch the overflow miracle manifest. OR, when You are saying–pause my child and take the rest I'm extending to you–as they go forth to cover and sacrifice for others, as Jesus did. Jesus is forever and always their Covering and their Sacrifice.

When my leaders feel they can't go anymore, thank You, Lord, for the overflow miracle and ability to go beyond, in You. Thank You for the overflow miracles that have been and will be birthed out of their obedience. And when you offer rest, thank You for their obedience, wisdom and discernment to receive the miracle of *rest* on every side, for You are God of *all*, in Jesus' Name!

Psalm 45:6; Revelation 19:16; Luke 4:8; Isaiah 47:4; John 14:6; Romans 6:23; 1 Corinthians 1:30; Matthew 10:20; Ephesians 2:14; Zephaniah 3:17; Ephesians 4:6; Psalm 150:1; Exodus 3:14; Revelation 4:8; Proverbs 3:13; Philippians 1:9; Revelation 3:22; Luke 5:5-6; Matthew 11:28-30;

Genesis 2:2-3; Luke 9:23-24; Hebrews 9:11-12; 1 Kings 2:3

Heart Notes, Insights, Revelations

_____

_____

_____

_____

_____

_____

_____

_____

_____

_____

_____

_____

_____

Heart Notes, Insights, Revelations

_____

_____

_____

_____

_____

_____

_____

_____

_____

_____

_____

_____

_____

Day 6: *Live Again!*

Praise and Worship:

As a song writer put it...*Father, Father, Father, we love You! Jesus, Jesus, Jesus, we praise You, Holy Spirit, YES, we adore You!*

I open this day of prayer, as always with praise and gratefulness in my heart–worshiping You in spirit and in truth! As I praise You Lord, I'm drawn to repentance, for You cannot dwell in a camp where there is sin, and I do not want to send up tainted worship to You.

I remove any sin that is creating a block to You hearing my prayers for Headship and Covering today.

Prayer:

I ask for forgiveness for sins I've committed knowingly and unknowingly. Reveal to me those sins I am not aware of, so I can bring them wholeheartedly before You. (Confess sins you are aware of and everything God is revealing now. Bring them before the Lord here.)

Father, I openly confess everything I've done that is not pleasing in Your sight. I know when I come in true repentance, Your Word says You are willing and just to forgive me. I ask for the strength and wisdom to avoid these same sins over and over. I put them under the Blood of Jesus and decree I am free and will not get entangled in the sins of old.

Thank You, Lord, for Your forgiveness. Thank You for another chance and Thank You for receiving my prayers on behalf of Your people, Your leaders.

I am calling Headship and Covering to live again and rise to their true, *new life* in Christ!

For in the beginning, the first breath of life, the first heartbeat, was given on the sixth day, the day of the creation of man. Jesus gave up His life on the sixth day, so the *new life* of man could be given. As today is the sixth day of prayer, I pray for Headship and Covering to breathe in new, resurrected life and to receive the new heartbeat that thrums to the rhythm of heaven! It beats with a heart of courage for holiness and righteousness; it beats to the syncopation of YOU!

In a newfound way, help them to recognize and perceive that the deepest needs and longings of their hearts are real and only found in Jesus. *You* put the longings in their hearts for the purpose of seeking You, because there is *more and there is another level they can go to–in You!* *Amen!*

Take them there, Lord, in the cleft of the Rock, in the Secret Place of the Most-High God, and minister unto them.

Lead them away, Holy Spirit, as you did with Jesus, to a quiet place where they can breathe You in deeply. For You are their very oxygen and You desire that they live again and rise to the *new* life and *new* level You have awaiting them! THERE'S MORE! There's always more in YOU. In Jesus' Name!

Song: Oxygen

By: Steffany Gretzinger

Psalm 100:4; John 4:24; Psalm 32:5; Psalm 5:4; Exodus 30:9; Psalm 66:18; Ephesians 1:7; Luke 12:2; James 5:16; Ephesians 6:10; James 1:5; Galatians 5:1; Psalm 9:1; 1 Timothy 2:2; 2 Corinthians 5:15; Genesis 1:26-27, 31; 1 Corinthians 15:45; John 11:25-26; Jeremiah 24:7; Psalm 107:9; Philippians 2:13; Psalm 42:7; Exodus 33:22; Psalm 91:1; Luke 5:15-16; Genesis 2:7; 1 Corinthians 2:9

Heart Notes, Insights, Revelations

_____

_____

_____

_____

_____

_____

_____

_____

_____

_____

_____

_____

_____

Heart Notes, Insights, Revelations

_____

_____

_____

_____

_____

_____

_____

_____

_____

_____

_____

_____

_____

Day 7: *Wait On the Lord, the Right Way*

Insight:

There are 'suddenly' blessings being prepared to break forth in our lives, but we must wait on the Lord the right way, with the right perspective, the right attitude and the right "heart" disposition.

When we wait the right way, at the appointed time, these blessings will "suddenly" happen and no demon in hell can stop this rush of the Spirit!

Praise and Worship:

Amazing Grace, how sweet the sound that saved a wretch like me, I once was lost, but now I'm found, was blind but now I see!

Thank You for saving me and opening my blind eyes!

You are a breath-providing God and You are breathtaking at the same time! Your love captivates my soul deep within! I live, move and have my being, in You.

Come, Lord Jesus, and take up residence in

me! God, I create a permanent place for You alone. A permanent home within me like the Shunammite woman did for the Prophet Elisha–a place of his own.

He didn't have to look for a place to stay when he visited Shunem–the double resting place– where the overflow of Your rest dwells and revives. It was already provided.

In like manner, God, You don't have to look for a place to stay. I want to be Your Shunem. I want Your double resting place to be within me.

Overflow with the double, in me! And not just for a visit Lord...live perpetually in me so I can pray forth Your heart, and Your will be done on earth, as it is in heaven!

Thank You, Lord, that I am assured that You hear me when I call!

Prayer:

Father, I pray for Headship and Covering to wait on You the right way. The world needs to witness this. You said..."Wait on the Lord and You will renew their strength"...While they're waiting, YOUR WAY, they will "mount up on wings like *eagles, they will run and not grow weary, they will walk and not faint."*

While they're in the midst of the battle, help them to praise You, serve You, honor You, WORSHIP YOU. I speak into their spirits TODAY, rise up! Don't wait until the battle is over, shout now!

Whatever the circumstances they're facing, whatever the condition, let this be their disposition: *"If God delivered me before, He'll do it again! I'm not waiting until the battle is over...I'm shouting to the Lord TODAY! I'm lifting my voice like a trumpet in Zion, for the JOY of the Lord is my strength!"*

For that is where the power is. That's where the breakthrough is. That's the place where 'suddenly' awaits!

We call it done by faith, in Jesus' Name!!!

Songs:

Wait On the Lord By Fred Hammond

Immediately By Tasha Cobbs

John 1:16; Psalm 33:6; Psalm 84:2; Acts 17:28; Ephesians 3:17-19; 2 Kings 4:9-10; John 12:49;

Tucked in HIM

Matthew 6:10; 1 John 5:15; Acts 2:2-3, 16:25 Psalm 27:14; Exodus 9:5; Habbakuk 2:3; John 17:23; Isaiah 40:31; Psalm 24:8-10; Isaiah 60:1-2; 2 Chronicles 20:17-24; Isaiah 58:1

Heart Notes, Insights, Revelations

Heart Notes, Insights, Revelations

_____

_____

_____

_____

_____

_____

_____

_____

_____

_____

_____

_____

_____

Day 8: *RECEIVE Rest*

Song: Something Happens

By: Preashea Hilliard

Insight:

The weight of being a leader in any realm can be overwhelming. Caring for the lives and souls of others can be a very daunting task, while putting the maintenance of our own souls on hold, is at risk.

This can wear leaders down. Therefore, we, the Body of Christ, must all be mindful of the work that is ours and that which is not...differentiating and discerning between the work that is ours and that which belongs to God.

It's easy to get the two mixed up and intertwined; it's a very fine line. When we get them mixed up, we bear too much and get worn down, leaving no energy for the work that really *is* ours, which can lead to giving out of the flesh, rather than an overflow from the Spirit.

When we operate this way, we ourselves, sometimes step into the role of the burden bearer and it's a job too big for any person's shoes to fill. Jesus is the only True Burden Bearer!

Praise and Worship:

Jesus, Jesus, Jesus, something happens, when we call on You!

This is my worship, Lord! I acknowledge that You are God and all I have to do is call on Your name—that powerful, miraculous name—in faith and even when I can't see it, something happens when I call You!

Prayer:

Today, I cover Headship and Covering in this place; to receive the rest that God is extending through Jesus, for His yoke is easy and His burden is light. You paid it all, Jesus, so I don't have to. I can rest in You.

Father, I come to you on behalf of my great leaders, for You said it is my duty to pray for those who have rule and authority over me, that it may be well with me.

In obedience to Your Word, I pray for

Headship and Covering to receive the gift of rest that You offer. I'm crying out for them to hear Your voice today. I bind all hindrances and distractions that would clog or clutter their ability to hear You.

Lord, help them to put away electronics, social media and *anything* else that appears to be innocent, but is a vampire sucking them dry, so they can *clearly* hear You.

Although the offer is there, they must know when and how to "receive" this rest, for the journey ahead is great and their energy must be reserved for when You tell them it is time to act.

I pray for a supernatural move of Your Spirit so they can clearly hear, and see, when You are speaking rest to their souls. Help them to know when to say yes and when to say no to others without any guilt attached.

Let Headship and Covering move synchronized, syncopated, in step and in sequence with the rhythm of heaven and fully receive their restoration through Your blessed rest. I decree fresh wind for their souls this day, in Jesus' Name. AMEN, SO BE IT!

Tucked in HIM

Romans 10:13; Philippians 2:9-10; Matthew 11:29; Galatians 3:13-14; 1 Timothy 2:2; Matthew 18:18; Hebrews 4:15-16; James 5:16; 1 Corinthians 10:13; Luke 10:38-42; Psalm 119:105; 1 Kings 19:7; Deuteronomy 5:33; Psalm 24:5; John 1:16

Heart Notes, Insights, Revelations

_____

_____

_____

_____

_____

_____

_____

_____

_____

_____

_____

_____

Heart Notes, Insights, Revelations

_____

_____

_____

_____

_____

_____

_____

_____

_____

_____

_____

_____

_____

Day 9: *Stop Running and Go on the Inward Journey*

Insight:

There are many assaults that come to wound Headship and Covering just because of the position, and power, they hold, to affect the lives of the people in their realm of influence, and even nations, for Jesus.

Many have allowed their flesh to die to some of those wounds and gotten a level of healing and deliverance, but there's another level of healing and deliverance waiting. Just because something is dead doesn't mean it can't cause harm.

Dead things, like a dead, dry branch amongst a lush living bush, are deceiving. Though it bears no fruit, just its existence still harnesses the power to poke, prod, cause scratches, scars and wounds to those who get close enough to them. For us, it's not enough for them to just die; they still **must be rooted out** and **burned**!

Dealing with wounds, especially ones that have been long gone, forgotten, and swept under the rug, is a painful process. Most people, including leaders, run from this place and just keep going and going.

They have so much responsibility and so much coming at them, that it's easier to keep it moving than it is to pause and process painful experiences. But not today!

This must be done in order for them to rise to the next level of healing, deliverance and glory in Christ. Today is the day of reckoning and going deep within, with JESUS as rear guard.

There is an emotional/physical connection in us, where the wounds of the soul drive the deeds that take place within the body, then manifests outwardly through our actions.

The Lord is trying to get us to take notice, recognize and deal with this. The way to clearly see what the Lord is bringing attention to in this deep area is to take the path less traveled. This path, or rather pilgrimage, will lead to someplace holy, which is deeper than most have gone before, and it's an individually wrapped journey. One can *only* take this intimate pilgrimage alone with Jesus, and that is the "Inward Journey" deep into the soul.

Praise and Worship:

I bless the name of Jesus in this moment. I pause and ponder You, meditating on You–Your goodness, Your kindness, Your holiness.

I ponder the person of Jesus–Your realness, Your compassion, Your heart–and I am in awe. I remain in awe of You, God! I take a moment to breathe You in deeply and listen for Your voice, to *Selah*–stop, pause and think about You!

When I think of You in this light, I am left speechless and humble in Your presence.

Prayer:

Today, I cry out in the Spirit for Headship and Covering to *stop* running from old pains and wounds, and dare to venture with Jesus into the depths of quietness, and to steal away with You, Lord, learning to practice Your presence. I usher them through prayer into that place in the realm of the spirit.

Oh GOD, people are waiting for them to line up with You for the next wave of Your glory! People's destinies are lying in the balance, waiting for Headship and Covering to steal away with You and *be healed,* so they can rise to the *new call,* the *new mandate* on their lives!

I usher them in the spirit, to take the road less traveled and *live* in Jesus, moment by moment. As they go inward, Jesus, You will shine outward even more!

Help them to go deeper in the wells of their souls, where there is peace, strength and stability untapped by most of this world. Lord, I pray for them to embrace this place where they can cry out to You about those things they don't want to face and haven't murmured to a soul.

You will answer and show them things which they do not know, and there You will *truly* heal the wounds they've been nursing for so long (thinking they've been fully healed).

But there's *more.* There's another level of healing, and there You will free the dead things that are clogging the spout of Living Water. In the name of Jesus, I root up, pluck out and burn these hidden enemies of the soul with the fire of the Holy Spirit! There will be no more trickles of Your Spirit.

By taking the journey inward, and letting You do the necessary work, this Living Water will gush *outward* and shift the world for the Kingdom into overflow, where the lame walk, the blind see, the sick are healed and the dead rise!

Lord, take them back to the beginning with You!

Let the Lord *arise* and let our enemies be scattered!

GOD'S Word to His People: *"Be Healed."*

GOD'S Word to Our enemies: *"Be Scattered."*

In JESUS' NAME, *"It is finished!"*

Song: Let It Happen

By: United Pursuit

Job 26:5; Isaiah 52:12; Psalm 143:5; Psalm 27:13; Psalm 36:7; 1 Peter 1:15-16; John 1:14; Hebrews 4:15; Luke 7:13; 1 John 4:10; Psalm 33:8; 1 Peter 5:6; Daniel 2:22; Psalm 64:6; Mark 6:31; Matthew 5:16; Exodus 33:14; Psalm 16:11; Isaiah 65:17; 3 John 1:2; Psalm 18:6; Jeremiah 33:3; Jeremiah 30:17; Malachi 4:2; John 7:38; Matthew 28:18-19; 2 Kings 3:17; Psalm 65:9; Psalm 65:12; Matthew 15:29-31; Matthew 10:7-8; Psalm 68:1; John 19:30

Heart Notes, Insights, Revelations

_____

_____

_____

_____

_____

_____

_____

_____

_____

_____

_____

_____

Heart Notes, Insights, Revelations

_____

_____

_____

_____

_____

_____

_____

_____

_____

_____

_____

_____

In Closing

You have completed 9 days of prayer for a leader or some leaders in your life. On behalf of our Lord and Savior, Jesus Christ, thank you! Thank you for the sacrifice of your time and partnering with God and being instrumental with His work in the earth.

Your prayers are critical, they are essential in this time and season and they work; they will bear much fruit. The effective prayer of a righteous man can accomplish much (*James 5:16 NASB*).

Be encouraged and know that you've accomplished much, and God is pleased with your efforts.

Now look for where God manifests peace in your life, because according to 1 Timothy 2:2 NLT, when you pray for those who are in authority, it results in peaceful and quiet lives marked by godliness and dignity. That's the God we serve.

When we are obedient and selflessly bless others, He blesses us! Thank You, Lord, You are worthy of all the praise, glory and honor!

Believe by faith, that what you have prayed is

done! Let's seal these prayers by faith in praise and worship to our Mighty God! **HALLELUJAH!!!**

Song: Lord You're Mighty

By: Youthful Praise

Heart Notes, Insights, Revelations

_____

_____

_____

_____

_____

_____

_____

_____

_____

_____

_____

_____

_____

_____

Heart Notes, Insights, Revelations

Salvation Prayer

It may be strange, but I don't assume that everyone who picks up a prayer book is saved. Just in case that's you, Jesus wants you to know that He loves you and died for your sins. He wants to re-shape and give you new life today and spend eternity in heaven with you.

Even if you've lived "like a Christian" but you know you've never confessed directly to Jesus and asked Him to come into your heart and life, this is for you. Don't go another day unsure of your standing in heaven. The rest of today is not promised, don't wait, give Him your life today!

If you are saved, maybe the prayer below can help you pray with, and lead, someone else into salvation.

Pray this genuinely from your heart. God will move and you can be assured that you are saved!

Scripture Reference:

Romans 10:9-11 (NASB) says that if you confess with your mouth Jesus as Lord, and believe in your heart that God raised Him from the dead, you will be saved; for with the heart a person believes, resulting in righteousness, and with the mouth he confesses, resulting in salvation. For the Scripture says, "Whoever BELIEVES IN HIM WILL NOT BE DISAPPOINTED."

Prayer:

Jesus, I confess with my mouth that You are Lord and I believe in my heart that God raised You from the dead. I confess that I am a sinner. I've messed up and I repent for everything I've done my own way, for every time I ignored and pushed You away. Thank You for loving me and dying for my sins.

Today, I give my whole life to You, Lord, I surrender. I ask You to come into my heart, take over my life, and teach me Your ways so I can live for You. Thank You for saving me.

In Jesus' Name, AMEN!

CONGRATULATIONS!!! Welcome to the family. You are saved!

Next Steps:

If you don't already have one, buy a bible that you can understand. There are many versions you can purchase or download, that are simple to read.

This is key, you must learn and know the Word of God for yourself!

If you are not already a part of a Bible-based church, seek one out. Pray and ask the Lord to simply show you where He wants you to go. It is there, in community, in family, that you'll grow in the things of the Lord with the support of like-minded people.

Until you find your church home, and after—especially after!—make a commitment to spend quiet, quality, time alone with God. For it is in solitude with Him you will find your identity, personal peace, and direction for your life.

Heart Notes, Insights, Revelations

Heart Notes, Insights, Revelations

_____

_____

_____

_____

_____

_____

_____

_____

_____

_____

_____

_____

About the Author

Keyon has been involved in ministry for over 17 years. Starting at Franklin Avenue Baptist Church in her hometown of New Orleans, Louisiana, she was active in teaching Sunday school, as well as involved in her church's dance ministry.

She married Dean Bernal Sr. in 2005 and moved to Lake Charles, LA, where she continues in dance ministry at United Christian Fellowship Church (UCF). There, the mantle of prayer passed on to her from her grandmother, has been nurtured and fed.

With a heart for God in everything she does, even her job as a fitness instructor turned into ministry as the Word of God began to pour out while teaching. She even began sharing a Word for the day, and praying at the end of her classes.

Eventually, the Lord shifted her to open her own fitness studio for a time, and, dedicated to encouraging and praying for others while getting them physically fit, became her work of ministry. She physically and spiritually trained and prayed with everyone that worked at Keyon's Fitness. Prayer circles and the Word of God were a regular part of daily operations at "KFit," as it was affectionately called by fellow instructors.

Because of all the different denominations of believers who came to work there, Keyon's Fitness was also coined, "the church without walls." Everyone was welcome.

Kingdom Business Kb was founded in 2017. Keyon accepted the call of the Lord to close Keyon's Fitness and step into a larger ministry which includes writing.

Keyon is currently the director for the youth dancers at UCF. She also works as choreographer director for local high schools in her area, where prayer circles begin every rehearsal and youths are taught the importance and power of prayer.

Keyon has been a guest speaker at several conferences and churches around the country. Returning from a recent pilgrimage to Israel, her heart is on fire with new depths and revelation in prayers she desires to share with you and the world. Prayer, studying, sharing the Word of God and the love of Jesus with others, are some of her greatest joys.

To order personalized or bulk copies of ***Tucked in HIM: 9 Days of Prayer for Headship and Covering***, Email Keyon at: <u>kingdombusinesskb@gmail.com</u> for pricing and shipping details.

Kingdom Business Kb

Made in the USA
Columbia, SC
27 July 2019